Ancient Shipwrecks

KC Smith

Franklin Watts
A Division of Grolier Publishing
New York • London • Hong Kong • Sydney
Danbury, Connecticut

To Elton, Alma, Corny, Beryl, Dean, Buzzy, Dana, and John.
Special thanks to Roger for his help with this project

Note to readers: Definitions for words in **bold** can be found in the Glossary at the back of this book.

Photographs ©: Art Resource, NY: 7 (Werner Forman Archive/The British Museum, London); Bridgeman Art Library International Ltd., London/New York: 32, 33 (AMQ104499/Sailing boat, copy of a wall painting, egg tempera on board, by Mrs Nina de Garis Davies/Ashmolean Museum, Oxford, UK.); Corbis-Bettmann: 3 bottom, 8 (Richard T. Nowitz), 10 (Vanni Archive); Institute of Nautical Archaeology: 14, 15, 19, 21, 22, 23, 44, 45, 47, 49, 50 (Don A. Frey), 12 (Peter Throckmorton), 16, 36, 38, 39, 41, 43, 48; Liaison Agency, Inc.: 52, 53 (X. Desmier/Rapho); Michael L. Katzev/Kyrenia Ship Excavation: 3 top, 24, 26, 27, 29; National Geographic Image Collection: 31 (Ira Block); Tony Stone Images: 4, 5.

Cover illustration by Greg Harris.

Visit Franklin Watts on the Internet at: http://publishing.grolier.com

Library of Congress Cataloging-in-Publication Data

Smith, KC
Ancient shipwrecks / KC Smith.
p. cm.— (Watts Library)
Includes bibliographical references and index.
Summary: Describes the development of underwater archaeology and the information it has discovered concerning early shipwrecks and their cultures.
ISBN 0-531-20381-6 (lib. bdg.) 0-531-16467-5 (pbk.)
1. Underwater archaeology—Juvenile literature. 2. Shipwrecks—Juvenile literature. [1. Underwater archaeology. 2. Shipwrecks.] I. Title. II. Series.
CC77.U5 S56 2000
910.4'52—dc21 99-055481

Printed in the United States of America.
1 2 3 4 5 6 7 8 9 10 R 09 08 07 06 05 04 03 02 01 00

Contents

Rough seas were among the many causes of shipwrecks throughout history.

Chapter One

Bathtub of Antiquity

"A storm burst while we were yet at sea, before we had reached land. . . . Then the ship perished, and of them that were on it not one survived. And I was cast on an island by a wave of the sea, and I spent three days alone . . . "

About 4,000 years ago, an unnamed sailor described the loss of his 180-foot (55-meter) vessel and 119 companions during a trading voyage from Egypt. While parts of his story are fanciful—for example, being rescued by a serpent covered with gold—the tale is one of the oldest known accounts of a shipwreck.

People have used watercraft for thousands of years to explore, colonize, trade, travel, and fight. In the course of these ventures, countless vessels have been lost at sea. Because every wreck is a puzzle-piece of history, underwater archaeologists study these remains to reconstruct a picture of the past.

In this book, we'll travel to the Mediterranean Sea, where very old and revealing shipwrecks have been discovered. We'll see how underwater archaeologists conduct their work and how their research has added to modern knowledge about ancient **cultures** and technology. But first, we should know something about the history of seafaring—travel by sea—in the region.

A Long Legacy

People stopped floating down waterways on logs when they learned to make dugout canoes, rafts of tree trunks or bundled reeds, and boats of animal skins. These methods, perhaps, are how mariners moved people and goods around the eastern Mediterranean more than 10,000 years ago. As the need for hardier craft arose, boats made of wooden planks were created. Early vessels were propelled by poles, paddles, and oars.

When sails were added, waterborne travel was revolutionized. We know about this innovation from two sources. The first is a model of a clay sailing boat from Mesopotamia (the ancient country located between the Euphrates and Tigris

The use of sails changed travel by water considerably.

Rivers in modern-day Iraq) dating back to 3500 B.C. The second is a picture of a boat with a sail painted on an Egyptian vase dating to 3100 B.C. When people learned to harness the wind, they discovered the most efficient way to transport anything anywhere.

What Does B.C. Mean?

B.C. is used with dates to indicate events before the time of Christ.

As sailors ventured farther from home, they cautiously kept coastlines in sight. However, as ships became sturdier and sea-

Ship in a Tomb

In 1952, Egyptian archaeologists found 1,224 pieces of a wooden ship in a sealed pit near the Great Pyramid of Giza. After each piece was recorded and **conserved,** the 140-foot (43-m) vessel was reconstructed (above). Marks carved by the ancient **shipwrights** that showed how the parts fit together helped this fourteen-year process. Built as a funeral barge for the Egyptian pharaoh Cheops (pronounced KEE-ops) in 2650 B.C., the Royal Ship of Cheops is the world's oldest surviving watercraft.

men grew bolder, they began to cross open water. They were guided by a map in the sky—the predictable positions of stars and the sun. By 3000 B.C., mariners were voyaging between Egypt and Crete, traveling the Aegean and Adriatic Seas, and traversing the Red Sea and Persian Gulf. Lively trade net-

Phoenicians

"Phoenicians" is the Greek name for the ancient people who lived along the coasts of modern-day Syria and Lebanon. They called their land Canaan and called themselves Canaanites.

works developed in the eastern Mediterranean as cargo ships moved from port to port. Around 1000 B.C., the Phoenicians (pronounced foe-NEE-shuns) expanded the horizon by exploring and settling the western end of the sea. Within 400 years, they had voyaged into the Atlantic Ocean and sailed around Africa.

The first guidelines for sailing in the Mediterranean were published around 350 B.C., but it was centuries before sea charts were common or accurate. To set their course, captains used stars, landmarks, wind direction, and personal experience. But even the best sailors encountered bad weather, treacherous coastlines, and pirates. Shipwrecks spanning thousands of years litter the Mediterranean, and many are within reach of modern-day scholars who study the past.

From Sponges to Science

Men have dived for sponges in the Mediterranean for 2,500 years. Simply by holding their breath, some divers could descend 200 feet (61 m). Occasionally, they encountered mounds of clay jars and other remains, but they didn't realize their significance. However, in 1900 when Greek sponge divers using modern equipment began to **salvage** an amazing

This dramatic statue of a young man—a god or a hero—was found near the Antikythera wreck.

cargo of bronze and marble statues, they caught the attention of archaeologists. A complex instrument with gears also was recovered, revealing that ancient people understood science and technology far better than scholars imagined. Dating to 80–70 B.C., the Antikythera (pronounced an-tee-KITH-er-a) wreck demonstrated that valuable clues to the past were waiting underwater.

In 1943, the aqualung—the first piece of modern **scuba** gear—was invented. Suddenly, anyone could explore the sea. Many wrecks in the Mediterranean Sea were looted by divers who had no interest in history. Moreover, divers unfamiliar with scientific techniques attempted to examine and **excavate** sites. It became clear that, for shipwrecks to be studied properly, archaeologists had to get off the boat and get into the water.

Where Is Antikythera?

Antikythera is an island between Crete and the Greek mainland. The first ancient shipwreck was discovered and studied there.

An archaeologist works around the brushwood packing material that lay in the bottom of the ship's hold at the Cape Gelidonya site in Turkey.

Chapter Two

Bronze-Age Bonanza

Underwater archaeologists study shipwrecks because they are time capsules of information about what a culture made, traded, ate, wore, worked with, and believed in. For centuries, ships were the most complex objects built in most societies, and seafaring embodied the most advanced knowledge of the day. While old records and artworks help to explain events and customs of the past, nothing is better than studying the actual evidence.

The Pioneering Effort

The discipline of underwater archaeology began in 1960 when George Bass led a three-month shipwreck project in Turkey at Cape Gelidonya (pronounced gel-e-DOH-nee-a), which means "cape of the swallows." It was the first time that trained archaeologists totally excavated a wreck on the seabed. Bass was an archaeology graduate student who learned to dive in order to direct the research. He was assisted by amateur archaeologist Peter Throckmorton, who had learned about the site from a sponge diver. Both men believed that excavation techniques used on land could be applied underwater. They went to Cape Gelidonya to test this idea.

The vessel had sunk near shore in 90 feet (27 m) of water. Because it landed on a rocky bottom with little protection from the environ-

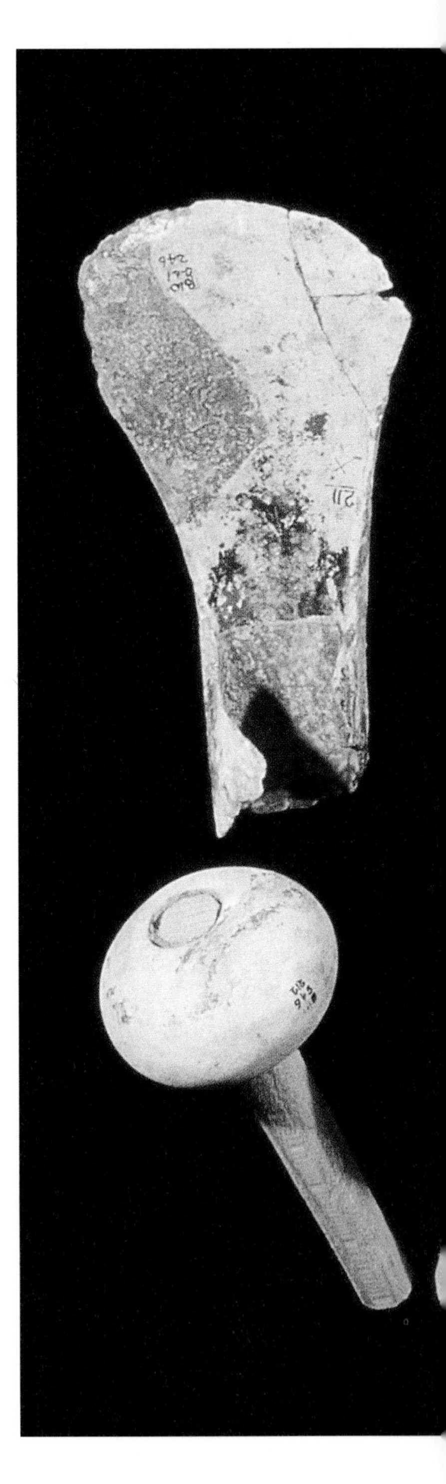

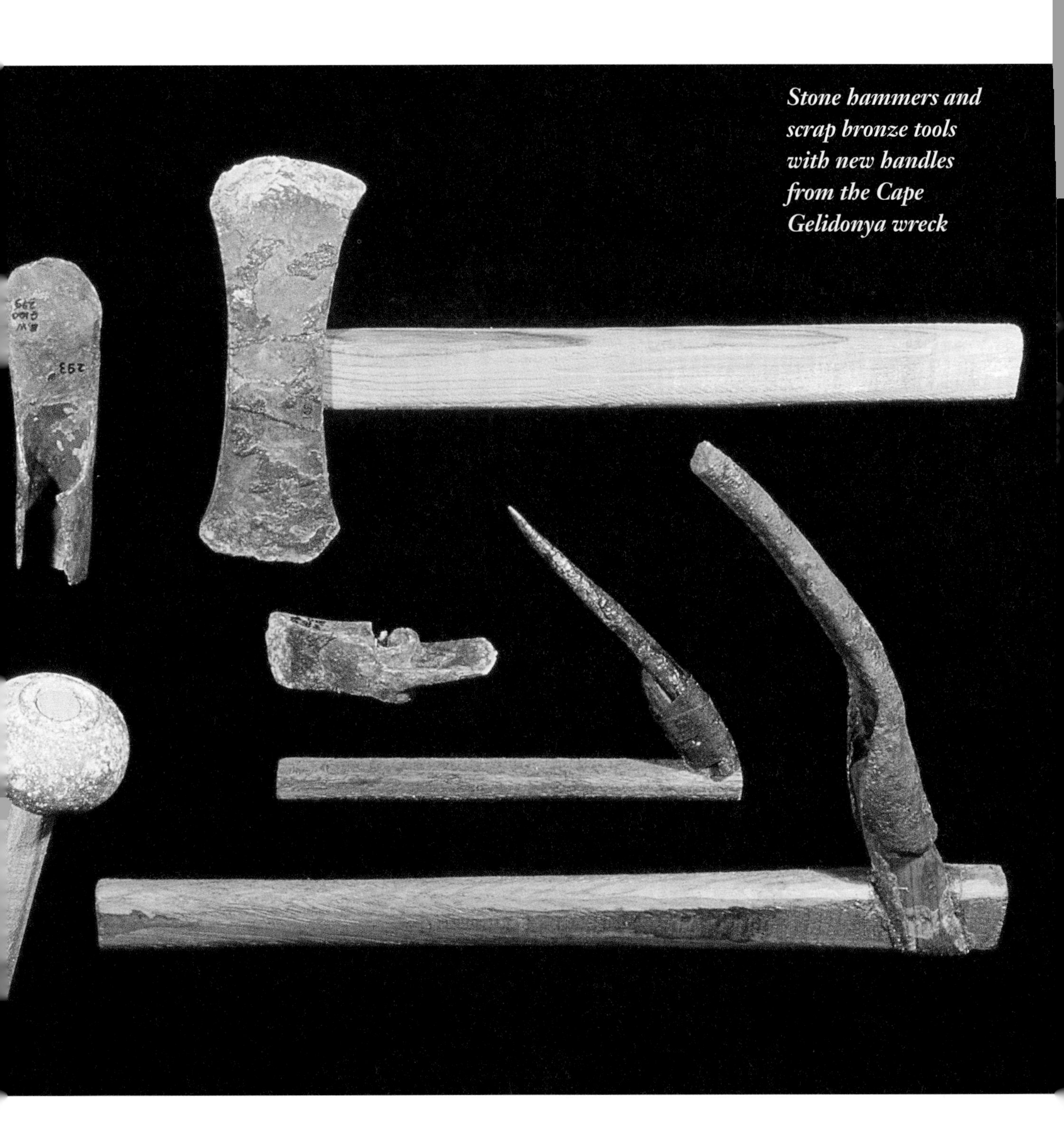

Stone hammers and scrap bronze tools with new handles from the Cape Gelidonya wreck

New Technology

Around 3000 B.C., tools and weapons made of bronze—a mixture of copper and tin—began to replace objects made of wood, bone, stone, and copper. This strong new metal revolutionized technology and culture. With better tools, shipwrights were able to build stronger vessels that carried larger cargoes over greater distances, which helped trade to expand. The Bronze Age lasted until 1050 B.C., when iron became the preferred metal.

Archaeologists have excavated two ships from the Late Bronze Age (1600–1050 B.C.) on the south coast of Turkey—one at Cape Gelidonya and one at Uluburun (pronounced oo-loo-BOO-roon). On both wrecks, the primary cargo consisted of metal **ingots**—copper and tin molded into convenient shapes for handling and transportation. Ingots were exchanged at trading centers and taken elsewhere to be made into bronze. The ingot shown above was recovered from the Uluburun wreck.

ment, the wooden **hull** had disintegrated. However, one ton of **artifacts** survived, including copper and tin ingots, broken and whole bronze tools, weapons and other objects, and personal possessions. Working from boats anchored over the wreck, team members removed sediments by fanning with their hands and using suction devices called airlifts. They mapped, measured, drew, and photographed the site before bringing anything to the surface. This careful recording allowed them to see where the cargo had been stored and where the crew had lived. Most objects were fused together by crusty marine deposits, so large clumps were raised and excavated at the team's camp on shore, where artifacts also were cleaned and documented. Today, these items are displayed at the Museum of Underwater Archaeology in Bodrum, Turkey.

A New Theory

After studying the artifacts and other evidence, Bass concluded that a small trading ship, 30 feet (9 m) long, sank about 1200 B.C. during a voyage from Syria and Palestine, on the eastern Mediterranean coast, to the island of Cyprus and points west. Someone on board was a traveling metalworker, who exchanged goods and services for raw materials (ingots) and scrap metal (broken tools). When Bass published this explanation, most scholars believed that Greeks in the western Mediterranean controlled the Late Bronze Age trade.

Research Support

In 1973, George Bass established an organization to support underwater archaeological research. Today, the Institute of Nautical Archaeology (INA) is based at Texas A & M University, where graduate students can train to become nautical archaeologists—people who specialize in the study of ships and seafaring.

INA has sponsored field projects worldwide on sites dating from 1350 B.C. to the nineteenth century.

However, evidence from the shipwreck, supported by artworks, documents, and archaeological sites from the era, showed that cultures in the East were just as influential.

Bass returned to Cape Gelidonya in the late 1980s with new tools and new research teams. Searching outside the original excavation area, archaeologists found artifacts and evidence overlooked during the first project. These new data confirmed some of Bass's original ideas, but they also caused him to reconsider others. Perhaps as important, because improved tools were available and some of Bass's own trained students participated, the second expedition showed that the young science of underwater archaeology was maturing nicely.

A Second Bronze-Age Wreck

In summer 1982, a sponge diver working at Uluburun—which means "grand cape"—on the south coast of Turkey noticed odd-shaped objects on the seabed. He described these "metal biscuits with ears" to his captain, who had seen a picture of a

Return visits to the Gelidonya site in the late 1980s located well-preserved wine jars.

metal ingot circulated by underwater archaeologists. The discovery was reported to the Bodrum Museum of Underwater Archaeology, where the Institute of Nautical Archaeology (INA) displays artifacts that it finds on ancient wrecks. Divers from the museum and INA examined the site. They quickly realized that a vessel with a huge cargo had wrecked in the fourteenth or thirteenth century B.C.

Directed by George Bass and Cemal Pulak, INA archaeologists spent a decade—from 1984 to 1994—excavating the Uluburun wreck. They made 22,412 dives on the wreck, totaling 6,613 hours underwater. Why did it take so long? One reason was the depth of the site. Wreckage was strewn along a rocky slope from 140 to 200 feet (43 to 61 m) long. Working at such depths is dangerous and difficult, and each diver could spend only twenty minutes twice a day on the seabed. In addition, excavation was conducted only in the summer, although artifact conservation and research continued year-round. But primarily the project took ten years because of the vast quantity of artifacts and ship remains—all of which the archaeologists wanted to recover.

Fabulous Finds

The main cargo consisted of eleven tons of metal ingots and one ton of tree sap used for incense, which was carried in nearly 150 clay jars. Other artifacts included ingots of glass, logs of ebony wood, ostrich eggshells, elephant tusks, hippopotamus teeth, and tortoise shells. The ship also carried

An ostrich egg recovered from the Uluburun wreck before (above) and after conservation

The Oldest Book

Researchers at Uluburun recovered the fragile remains of the oldest book ever found, consisting of two wooden tablets joined by ivory hinges.

huge ceramic jars filled with smaller pottery, drinking cups in the shape of a ram's head, thousands of beads, ivory cosmetics containers, gold and silver jewelry, tools and weapons, oil lamps, metal cauldrons and bowls, and stone anchors. There was also evidence of twelve different food items. Below this mass of cargo and crew's possessions lay the remains of the wooden hull. Enough of the 50-foot (15-m) ship survived for archaeologists to understand how the vessel had been constructed.

When the Uluburun ship sank around 1350 B.C., it was a staggering loss to the owners and merchants, but it was a treasure trove for modern archaeologists. The oldest shipwreck excavated underwater, it contained one of the largest collections of ancient trade goods. The vessel probably began its voyage in Syria, Palestine, or Cyprus, but by the time it sank, it had acquired artifacts from eleven different cultures. This rich and diverse cargo proves that widespread trade existed and that seafarers from the eastern Mediterranean played a major role in the network.

Opposite: Researchers study a large elephant tusk cut at both ends.

Kyrenia II, *a full-scale replica of the ship excavated at Kyrenia*

Chapter Three

From Seabed to Sea Trials

The *Kyrenia II* sailed grandly up the Hudson River in New York amid the other Tall Ships in the 1986 Fourth of July parade. An odd-looking watercraft, with one broad sail and two eyes painted on the bow, it was a full-scale replica of a vessel that sank twenty-two centuries ago during the time of Alexander the Great. It also was an example of "experimental archaeology"—a process in which modern researchers reproduce an object to learn how it was made and used.

Storage Jars of Antiquity

For centuries, wet and dry goods were shipped in pottery jars called amphoras. With two handles and a pointed base, their shape made them easy to transport. When found on the seabed, amphoras are a good indication of a wreck. Because potters often stamped them with their own unique mark, their origin can be traced. In addition, the style and shape of these jars evolved over time. Knowing the amphoras' origin and when the various types were in use helps archaeologists to reconstruct cargoes and trade routes in different periods of history.

Amphoras and Almonds

Searching in 100 feet (31 m) of water near Kyrenia, Cyprus, in 1965, a Greek sponge diver noticed a pile of pottery jars called **amphoras** on the sandy, grass-covered seabed. When he surfaced, a storm had come up, so he had no time to record the site's position. But after relocating it two years later, he shared his secret with archaeologist Michael Katzev, who was leading a shipwreck survey in Cyprus for the University of Pennsylvania Museum.

The amphora pile on the seabed was a mere 10 by 16 feet (3 by 5 m). Suspecting that additional remains might be

Underwater amphora pile at the Kyrenia site

buried, Katzev's team conducted mechanical and electronic tests and discovered that the site actually was three times that size. Because the wreck was undisturbed and largely unexposed, the prospects were very good that hull remains might exist. An expert who examined the amphoras dated them to the fourth century B.C.

Under Katzev's direction, archaeologists began a two-year excavation in 1968. About 400 amphoras, nearly 10,000 almonds, pottery, food-grinding stones, bronze coins, iron ingots, ship's equipment, foodstuffs, and other items were recorded and recovered. The artifacts suggested that the wreck occurred around 300 B.C. Four sets of eating utensils and cups from the island of Rhodes indicated the size and possible home port of the crew.

Archaeologists were mystified by the absence of other personal possessions, however. A possible explanation emerged after eight encrusted objects were cleaned. The artifacts were iron spearpoints, several of which had been found embedded in the outside of the hull. This clue led Katzev to conclude that pirates had attacked the ship and seized the crew, their belongings, and other valuable items before sinking the craft to hide their crime.

Reconstructing the Hull

About 75 percent of the hull lay buried below the cargo. Archaeologists spent five years recovering, conserving, and studying more than 5,000 pieces of waterlogged wood. They

The reconstructed Kyrenia wreck is on display in Cyprus.

Wood Conservation

Waterlogged wood must be soaked in wax or another preservative to restore its strength and ensure its preservation.

reassembled the pieces exactly as they were found on the seabed. Today, the reconstructed ship is displayed in the Crusader Castle in Kyrenia.

To understand the vessel's design and prepare for the reconstruction, INA ship reconstructor J. Richard Steffy created miniature models of the wreck. These models enabled him to design a small replica, which his teenage sons sailed to test the ship's seaworthiness. Steffy learned that the Kyrenia ship had been built by the "shell-first" method: an outer shell of hull **planks** was erected and then interior **frames** were added. The planks were held together by wooden wedges called **tenons** that fit into slots called **mortices** that were cut into the top and bottom edges of hull planks. Shell-first, mortice-and-tenon ship construction was used from at least 1350 B.C. to the fourth century.

So much information was acquired about the Kyrenia ship's construction that INA researchers, with support from the Hellenic Institute for the Preservation of Nautical Traditions, decided to build a full-scale replica. A Greek boatbuilder near Athens volunteered his shipyard for the project. For three years, shipwrights painstakingly assembled a copy of the 45-foot (14-m) vessel. As much as possible, they used the techniques, materials, and replicas of the tools that the ancient builders had used.

Finally, on June 22, 1985, the *Kyrenia II* was launched during a celebration in Athens. It was later shipped to New York

Shipwrights used original techniques to build the Kyrenia II.

for the Tall Ships parade. Since that time, it has visited major ports in Greece and Cyprus and has duplicated part of the final, fatal voyage of its namesake.

Studying ancient ships provides a wealth of information about past cultures.

Chapter Four

Unique Techniques

Because ships moved people and goods from place to place, they are a key to understanding how past cultures interacted and survived. Unfortunately, nature and time usually destroy wooden vessels on the seabed. When hull remains are encountered, archaeologists record and study every detail—sometimes using innovative measures—to learn how the watercraft was designed, built, used and sailed.

Wine for Rome

By the first century B.C., the Roman Republic, centered in modern-day Italy, ruled the Mediterranean Sea. Initially, Romans were not seafarers, but a series of wars prompted them to develop a navy. This led to the construction of large merchant vessels to import building materials, luxury items, and amphoras filled with food and wine.

In 1967, French navy divers spotted a pile of amphoras camouflaged by marine grass off the port of La Madrague, near Toulon, France. Although the site was only 60 feet (18 m) deep, its location and grassy cover had protected it from looters. The navy used a sophisticated metal detector called a magnetometer to determine the size of the wreck. The buried

Recovering amphoras from the Madrague de Giens wreck in France

vessel was more than 130 feet (40 m) long and nearly 40 feet (12 m) wide—one of the largest ancient wrecks yet discovered.

André Tchernia and Patrice Pomey, French archaeologists from the Centre National de la Recherche Scientifique and the Université de Province, directed the excavation of the Madrague de Giens wreck from 1972 to 1982. A Roman ship that sank in 75–60 B.C., it contained nearly 6,500 wine amphoras and a cargo of other ceramics. Potters' marks on the amphoras allowed researchers to identify their exact place of manufacture in Italy.

As archaeologists removed seabed sediments, rows of amphoras stacked 10 feet (3 m) high were mapped with a unique system of photography before being recovered. Below the cargo, extensive hull remains were found. After recording them on the seabed, researchers used underwater chain saws to remove sections of the vessel, which they studied on land and later replaced and reburied. This unusual process allowed them to draw a detailed plan of the hull and to learn how large Roman merchant ships were built during the peak of shell-first boat construction.

Easy Descent

Archaeologists found stones on the site that ancient divers carried to help them sink while recovering cargo from the wreck.

A Boat from Christ's Time

During a drought in 1986, the Sea of Galilee (also called Lake Kinneret) in Israel was lower than usual, and the bottom was visible. Two fishermen noticed the outline of a sunken craft and reported their discovery. Archaeologist Shelley Wachsmann from the Department of Antiquities and Museums sur-

Researchers transported the Kinneret boat from the excavation site to the conservation location in a protective wrapping.

veyed the site and found the lower hull of an ancient boat in good condition. Artifacts around the wreck dated from the first century B.C. and the first century A.D. Because the craft was similar to boats described in the Bible, the media speculated that Jesus and his disciples might have used the vessel as they fished and preached at Galilee. This attention threatened the vessel's safety, so an emergency excavation was undertaken.

A dam, or enclosure, was constructed around the wreck, and the water inside was pumped out. The boat was excavated, recorded, and studied in place. It then was wrapped in a cocoon of fiberglass frames and plastic foam. The dam was reflooded, and the boat was floated to shore, where it was placed in a special conservation tank. Today, the cleaned and treated vessel can be seen in a museum at nearby Kibbutz Ginosar at Galilee.

What Does A.D. Mean?

A.D. is used with dates to indicate events after the birth of Christ. It stands for the Latin words *Anno Domini*, "in the year of the Lord."

Well-Used Vessel

Measuring 27 by 7.6 feet (8 by 2 m), the Kinneret boat was constructed in the shell-first method. It had been repaired several times, and when it was found, several important parts were missing. After INA ship reconstructor J. Richard Steffy studied the remains, he concluded that the small fishing and transport vessel was abandoned after a long life of use—but only after certain pieces were removed to serve as "spare parts" for newer craft. Remains of other boats nearby suggested that the area may have been used for shipbuilding and repair in ancient times.

The island of Yassi Ada, which means "flat island" in Turkish

Chapter Five

Ancient Ship Trap

There are places in the sea that are traps for passing ships. The island of Yassi Ada (pronounced YAH-suh AH-duh) off the southern coast of Turkey is an example. More than a dozen wrecks spanning twenty-two centuries are visible on the seabed. Three sites have been excavated by underwater archaeologists, and two of these have provided valuable clues about the evolution of nautical technology.

Fourth-Century Wreck

In the late fourth century, a Roman merchant vessel sank off Yassi Ada in 120 to 140 feet (37 to 43 m) of water. Archaeologists worked on the site in 1967, 1969, and 1974, although they did not excavate it entirely. Nonetheless, they found a cargo of 1,100 amphoras, utilitarian items such as pottery and lamps, crew's possessions, and evidence of the kitchen, or galley. The surviving hull remains revealed that the 62-foot (19-m)-long vessel had been built by the shell-first method. However, there were variations in the usual shell-first construction pattern. These variations suggested to archaeologists that, by this point in history, shipbuilding techniques were changing.

Seventh-Century Wreck

By the seventh century A.D., the Byzantine Empire encompassed much of the Mediterranean Basin. To maintain its power, it relied on a strong navy and a state-owned commercial fleet. However, officials eventually realized that it was more efficient to have private ship owners import and export goods. Around A.D. 625, one of these merchants, a man called Georgios, lost a ship carrying 900 amphoras of wine off Yassi Ada. From 1961 to 1964, his misfortune became the object of an excavation conducted by archaeologists from the University of Pennsylvania Museum and led by George Bass.

Resting on a slope in 105 to 128 feet (32 to 39 m) of water, the cargo was coated with marine growth, which archaeologists

Trend-Setting Techniques

Archaeology is a destructive science. To understand a site thoroughly, archaeologists dismantle the deposits layer by layer. On land, usually everything is removed. Underwater, researchers often excavate down to the hull, which they study but leave in place because of the difficult and costly process of recovering and conserving wooden remains. In each case, every layer is measured, mapped, and recorded so that a plan of the site can be drawn and details can be reconstructed later.

On the seventh-century wreck at Yassi Ada on the south coast of Turkey, archaeologists experimented with a variety of techniques to improve their ability to record details. Not only did they adapt tools normally used on land, but they also developed new ways to map and photograph the remains. This careful documentation revealed subtle information about the ship and the crew. Many of the methods they developed are now standard underwater archaeological techniques, and some have been improved even further.

removed with scrub brushes before labeling every object. The wreck was mapped and photographed, and a small section of amphoras was removed to see how they were stacked and whether wood existed below—and it did. During four seasons, researchers painstakingly recorded and removed amphoras, anchors, food containers and cooking utensils, coins, and other artifacts, evidence of the ship's galley, and hull remains. The excavated items were taken to Bodrum Castle in Turkey, where they were conserved, documented, and analyzed.

What's for Dinner?

Not enough of the wooden hull survived to merit reconstructing the remains on land. However, it was possible to create very accurate models, especially of the stern, or back end of the ship, where the galley was located. Although the ship was rather small—about 67 feet (20 m) long—it had a well-equipped cooking and storage area. More than sixty pots, jars, jugs, and pitchers, as well as four or five sets of tableware, were found around the tiled firebox, or hearth, which had an iron grill and a tiled roof. Food and special utensils were kept in a locked cabinet nearby, along with coins, tools, lamps, and other objects. An inscription on a weighing device found in the locker revealed that Georgios, the captain, also was a Christian church official.

Elsewhere on the wreck, eleven iron anchors were found—some ready for use and others stacked as spares. The ship also carried about 900 amphoras of various shapes and sizes. On this voyage, most had been filled with wine, although carved inscriptions on some of the jars indicated that they previously had stored other items and had different owners. Nonetheless, the amphoras were a clue to the purpose of the voyage. The Byzantine Empire at this time was engaged in a war so costly that the church had to help supply the army. Based on the cargo and other artifacts, and the fact that the ship could feed so many people, archaeologists surmised that the craft was owned by the church and was supporting the war effort.

In addition, after studying the scant but revealing hull remains, researchers could see that shipbuilding techniques were evolving. The shell-first method had been used in the lower part of the hull, but in the upper part, frames were inserted before the outer planks were added. The reasons for this change are unclear; however, shipwrights seemed to be learning that the complex and labor-intensive shell-first method was not necessary to build a sturdy ship. As we shall see, they eventually abandoned shell-first, mortice-and-tenon construction entirely for the modern "frame-first" method.

Divers use a lifting cradle and lifting balloons to bring the amphoras to the surface.

After an underwater site has been excavated, conservators begin painstaking work in the laboratory.

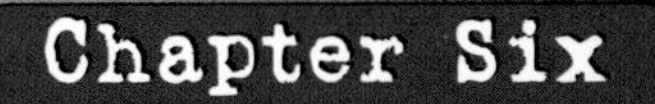

Chapter Six

Cargo of Glass

Underwater archaeologists often say that for every month they work in the field, they spend at least two years in the laboratory and library. The real process of archaeology takes place in these land-based locations, where the raw evidence from a shipwreck is conserved, studied, analyzed, researched, reconstructed, and explained. Archaeologists know that for every question they answer, two or three new questions will arise.

Missing Link

By A.D. 700, Muslims—followers of the religion of Islam—controlled the eastern and southern Mediterranean. The Byzantine Empire maintained its hold on the northern shores. Hostilities and naval engagements between the two powers disrupted traditional trade patterns for centuries, although some commercial interaction continued.

Great Sites

The best wrecks provide new knowledge about the history of seafaring, not necessarily the most artifacts.

Relations eventually improved, and a peace treaty was signed in 1027. Written information about seafaring during this era existed in historical documents, but no information was available about how ships were constructed. Thus, when George Bass was shown a wreck that seemed to date from the period, he was excited by the prospect of filling the missing gap. In addition, the vessel appeared to have a rather unique cargo.

The ship sank in the harbor of Serçe Limani (pronounced SAIR-chey lee-MAN-ee)—which means "sparrow harbor"—on the south coast of Turkey. Archaeologists believe one of its anchors broke, and it was driven by wind onto rocks near shore. It came to rest in about 110 feet (34 m) of water on a flat area of sand. A Turkish sponge diver took Bass to the site in 1973 during a shipwreck survey that the Institute of Nautical Archaeology (INA) conducts annually to locate new sites. When archaeologists inspected the wreck at Serçe Limani, they found the seabed littered with amphoras and hundreds of brightly colored pieces of glass.

Hazards and Intrigues

With Turkish government approval, Bass returned in 1977 to begin a project that lasted three years. To prepare for the excavation, his INA team placed a metal framework, or grid, over the remains to help with the mapping. By now a common device in shipwreck research, the grid enabled divers to keep track of what was found in various squares on the site.

The team also installed an underwater "telephone booth," developed on Bass's earlier projects. This metal structure, topped with a wide, plastic dome, had air hoses and a communications line connected to the surface. As many as four divers could stand inside, dry from the chest up, to talk with one another and people in the boat above. Topside, the team set up a recompression chamber to treat suspected cases of "the bends," a potentially fatal diving condition. But these recording and safety features had no effect on a hazard created by the ship's cargo—inevitable cuts on

Archaeologists used a rigid metal grid to help map the Serçe Limani wreck.

An airspace within the plexiglass dome of the "telephone booth" allows a diver to communicate with the people on the surface.

the divers' hands as they excavated more than three tons of broken glass.

One of the larger cargoes on board, the glass took several forms. Amazingly, more than eighty cups, tumblers, bottles, and bowls survived the sinking intact. Reflecting a stunning array of shapes, sizes, and decorative patterns, these fragile artifacts probably were packed in wicker baskets or crates and represented special items for trade. In addition, raw glass called **cullet** was found: about two tons of large, manageable chunks, and nearly a million shards, or pieces, of glassmaking waste and glass vessels that were already broken when loaded on board in baskets. Produced in an Islamic factory near the Syrian coast, the cullet was destined for an unknown glassworks elsewhere, to be melted and fashioned into new objects.

However, a different fate awaited the shards once they were excavated. In a remarkable exercise of patience and artifact reconstruction, archaeologists sorted the broken fragments—representing 10,000 to 20,000 different vessels—by color, shape, thickness, and pattern. Shards with similar features were compared to see whether they fit together. Through this process, hundreds of items of glassware have been reassembled, and some have shapes that have never been seen before.

Surviving Tradition

The art of fine glassmaking virtually ceased in Europe between the sixth and thirteenth centuries, but it was kept alive elsewhere by Muslim artisans. They made glass by mixing soda, sand, lime, and a small amount of cullet. Minerals were added to create color. Analysis of artifacts from the wreck at Serçe Limani indicates that they came from the same source, which means that they probably were picked up at one port. However, the name of that port remains a mystery.

Cautious Commerce

In keeping with economic trends of the time, the Serçe Limani wreck, also called the Glass Wreck, carried several different cargoes. This diversity protected merchants from unexpected changes in the price of goods. In addition to glass, a variety of Islamic ceramics was found, including cooking pots, baking dishes, jugs, bowls, and **gargoulettes**—one-handled jugs with a built-in filter. One hundred and ten Byzantine amphoras were recovered. Some probably contained provisions for the crew, but most no doubt were filled with marketable wine.

Equally intriguing were the cargoes that seemed to be missing. To sail properly, a ship must be ballasted, or balanced, with weight in its lower hull. On the Serçe Limani wreck, rocks, cullet, and other cargo provided some of this ballast. However, very little material was found in one area of the site. Researchers believe that a cargo recently had been unloaded or that perishable items had been stored there.

Personal gear carried on the ship found in the harbor of Serçe Limani included scissors and a wooden comb.

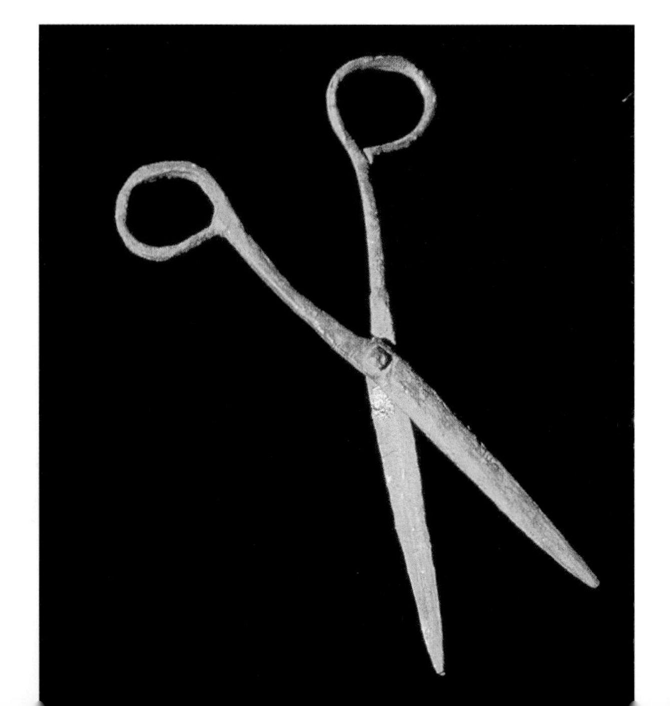

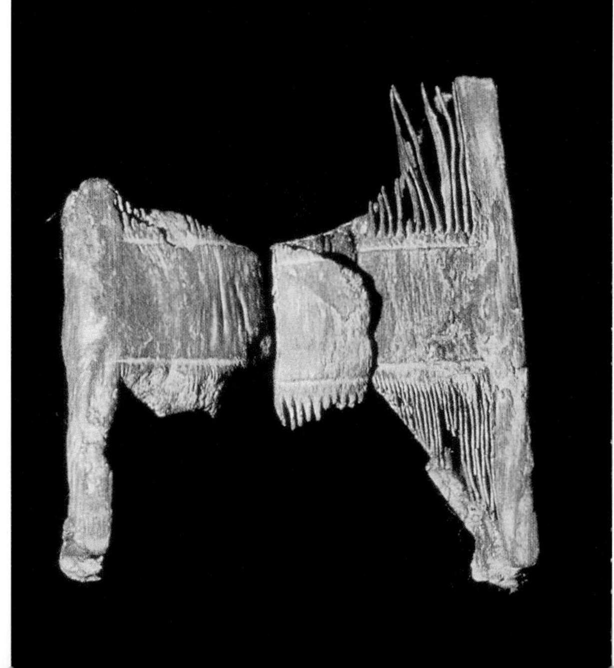

In an area of the wreck where intact glassware was discovered, a cache of personal possessions turned up. These included glass weights, cooking pots, and a toilet kit with scissors, a razor, a wooden comb, and Byzantine copper coins. Pork bones in one of the pots suggested that the owner was a Christian, since Muslims were forbidden to eat pork.

When and Where?

To determine the age of the wreck, INA archaeologists used several clues. Byzantine coins ranged from 970 to 1030, and Islamic glass weights bore dates from 1021/22 or 1024/25. Thus, they concluded that the ship sank in the third decade of the eleventh century. Pinpointing its origin and route was more difficult because of the mixture of Byzantine and Islamic artifacts. The ship and crew seem to have originated in Turkey's Sea of Mamara, just south of Constantinople, the capital of the Byzantine Empire. After trading at Islamic ports on the southeastern Mediterranean coast, it was lost on its voyage home.

If the Serçe Limani wreck artifacts were revealing to archaeologists, so were the wooden remains of the 50-foot (15-m)-long vessel. Although only 20 percent of the hull survived, researchers learned that the ship exemplified a new ship construction. Rather than building a shell of hull planks first, the shipwrights had created an internal skeleton formed by the **keel** and frames, and then added the outer skin. This frame-first method is still used today. Thus, when it was found, this wreck was the oldest known example of modern ship construction.

Technological innovations are providing fascinating opportunities for the growing field of underwater archaeology.

Chapter Seven

Wider Horizons

Forty years of experience and innovation have moved underwater archaeology from the fringes of the ocean into the deep sea. Today, scientists use vehicles controlled from the decks of research vessels to find and record the broken hulls and lost cargoes of sunken ships thousands of feet below. For example, in 1985 a French and American expedition located and photographed the famous ocean liner *Titanic* at a depth of 12,450 feet (3,797 m) in the north Atlantic. In

1998, with National Geographic Society support, an expedition found the World War II aircraft carrier USS *Yorktown* on the floor of the Pacific at a depth of 16,650 feet (5,078 m).

Adapted from other scientific fields such as marine geology and biology, the tools used to search the deep ocean are providing new opportunities to explore ancient shipwrecks. In addition to locating, recording, and mapping a site, remotely operated vehicles, or ROVs, can retrieve artifacts and bring them to the surface for archaeologists to examine. Recent Mediterranean projects have employed a small nuclear-powered research submarine, supplied by the U.S. Office of Naval Research, which can carry scientists into deep water to investigate shipwrecks firsthand.

Thanks to deep-sea technology, a new era of discovery is dawning for underwater archaeology. In a mere century, the study of ancient shipwrecks has advanced from haphazard finds made by sponge divers to sophisticated scientific study of lost ships on the floors of the world's oceans and seas. With this promising future, now is a good time for young explorers to think about becoming marine archaeologists.

Glossary

amphoras—ancient Greek pottery jars or vases

archaeology—the scientific study of past cultures based on artifacts and other evidence left behind

artifacts—objects made or modified by humans

conservation—the documentation, analysis, cleaning, and treatment of an artifact to ensure its survival

cullet—raw glass

cultures—the institutions, tools, customs, rituals, and beliefs of a group of people

excavate—to scientifically recover and study the remains of past human activity

frames—wooden structures that branch outward and upward from a ship's keel

gargoulettes—one-handled jugs with a built-in filter

hull—the body of a ship

ingots—copper, tin, or bronze molded into convenient shapes for handling and transportation

keel—the backbone of a ship

mortices—slots cut into the top and bottom edges of hull planks, in which tenons were wedged to hold the planks together

planks—long, thick, wooden boards that form the outside skin of a ship

salvage—to save from wreckage

scuba—(Self-Contained Underwater Breathing Apparatus); modern diving equipment

shipwrights—people who build or repair boats

tenons—wooden wedges that fit into slots cut into the top and bottom edges of hull planks

To Find Out More

Books

Lerner Geography Department. *Sunk! Exploring Underwater Archaeology*. Minneapolis: Runestone Press, 1994.

Macaulay, David. *Ship*. Boston: Houghton Mifflin Company, 1993.

Platt, Richard. *Shipwreck*. New York: Alfred A. Knopf, 1997.

Schultz, Ron, Nick Gadbois, and Peter Aschwanden. *Looking Inside Sunken Treasure*. Santa Fe: John Muir Publications, 1993.

Tritton, Roger, ed. *The Visual Dictionary of Ships and Sailing*. New York: Dorling Kindersley, 1991.

Organizations and Online Sites

Archaeological Institute of America
656 Beacon Street
Boston, MA 02215–2010
http://www.archaeological.org/
This website offers up-to-date information about the archaeology profession.

British Sub-Aqua Club
Telford's Quay
Ellesmere Port, South Wirral
Cheshire L65 4FY, England
http://www.bsac.com/
This website provides information about learning to dive.

Institute of Nautical Archaeology
P.O. Drawer HG
College Station, TX 77841–5137
http://nautarch.tamu.edu/ina/
This website provides information about the institute's projects.

Nordic Underwater Archaeology
Per Åkesson, editor
http://www.abc.se/~m10354/uwa/index.html
This website focuses on underwater sites in northern Europe.

A Note on Sources

Writing *Ancient Shipwrecks* was a challenge because it required historical information that was new to me. So I approached the project in the same way that one writes a term paper. I made an outline and decided which shipwrecks to describe. I shared my ideas with experts to be sure that I was on the right track. And then I began to gather research materials.

Some of the books and articles that I needed were available among the resources that my husband and I have collected over the years. However, to get the most up-to-date information, I went to the library to look for recent publications, and I searched the Internet for reports about the projects I was describing. I did a lot of reading before I began to write, and I kept stacks of resources handy so I could check and compare facts as I worked. When the manuscript was completed, I sent it to several underwater archaeologists to read to be sure that I had presented the details accurately.

—KC Smith

Index

Numbers in *italics* indicate illustrations.

About the Author

Since 1976, KC Smith has worked on underwater archaeological projects in the United States, the Caribbean, and Africa. As program supervisor at the Museum of Florida History in Tallahassee, she develops educational programs about history, archaeology, and folklife. KC Smith is a charter member of the Society for American Archaeology Public Education Committee and coedits its publication, *Teaching with Archaeology*. She has also edited the Institute of Nautical Archaeology newsletter.

KC Smith has studied humanities, archaeology, and history at Florida Atlantic University, Texas A & M University, and Florida State University. Her interest in shipwrecks comes from helping her husband Roger, an underwater archaeologist, with research projects. She believes that the findings from such projects should be shared with the public, especially young people. KC Smith is the author of the Watts Library books *Exploring for Shipwrecks* and *Shipwrecks of the Explorers.*